THE USER MANUAL OF ME

USE NEUROSCIENCE TO CREATE A PERSONAL BRAND STATEMENT THAT BUILDS TRUST

By

DAVID C WINEGAR

Copyright © 2020

Table of Contents

About the Author

David C Winegar is an author, trainer, coach, speaker, and applied neuroscience advocate who travels the world helping organizations and individuals to achieve more through a better understanding of human behavior. His work has taken him to four continents, coaching 1 000s of people from over 70 countries.

Before getting his MBA in organizational behavior and eBusiness from the University of Pittsburgh, he had a diverse work background including; working at the Smithsonian Institution's American History Museum, at the National Archives of the United States of America as a top-secret records declassification expert, and an international teacher of history and geography in Helsinki, Finland.

Since receiving his MBA in 1995, he has been in no less than six tech start-up companies, 3 in the US and 3 in Finland, including a forerunner to Twitter and one of the first mobile email services. For the last 11 years, he has been running his organizational development and coaching consulting firm, Absolute-North Ltd., which uses the latest psychological and neuroscience research to develop people. He has developed an experiential learning method called Artificial Experience Building, which uses neuroscience-backed research to better commit learning to long-term memory.

He is the author of two books on applied neuroscience, _Brainsights_, and _The Elevator Pitch of You_, both available worldwide in electronic and print formats at your favorite bookstores.

4

David's work has been in a broad spectrum of industries, everything from mobile gaming, and SAS companies, to industrial equipment, shipping, and machinery.

David's LinkedIn Profile:
https://www.linkedin.com/in/davidwin/

Absolute-North's Corporate Site:
 http://absolute-north.com/

He currently lives in Helsinki, Finland.

INTRODUCTION

We all have heard of and used "user manuals." A user manual is a document to assist a user in using and working with a piece of equipment or software product. They are developed to guide the user so that they will have less problems and be more successful in using the product.

One of the determining factors in working with other people successfully is in getting to know them. Understanding what "makes them tick." What they value, and how they like to work are important factors in understanding what you can do to work better together.

We normally don't spend a lot of time in getting to know the people we work with and given the brain's proclivity for making quick assumptions we often get it wrong. Our brain imagines things that are not there. It creates stories based on the wrong interpretation of events that leads to negative and destructive feelings. This can all be avoided if we take the time to open the channels of communication about who we are.

What if every person came with a user manual? A guide that explains who they are and how to work with them? A few words that would provide insight into who they are and what you can do to connect with them better. The opportunity for creating greater understanding and opening productive, and transformational conversations, then becomes more possible. Better conversations lead to better relationships. Better relationships allow an environment of innovation and productivity.

Trustful relationships in teams are at the foundation of psychologically safe work places. The latest research shows a direct correlation between trust and performance.

The User Manual of Me online tool and companion workbook's purpose is to assist you in a personal brand statement to help others understand who you are, what you value, and how you like to work. It shows you how to construct a personal leadership brand statement according to the latest neuroscience research that has been proven to connect with people better.

A well-crafted leadership band statement's purpose is to evoke positive emotions, thoughts, and images in people. To help you connect with others on a personal level and open the channels of communication about what is important and valuable in working better together.

NOTICE OF COPYRIGHT

UNDERSTANDING THE BRAIN AND HOW IT PROCESSES INFORMATION

Neuroscientist now are confident in their understanding of the functional areas of the brain. The rapid advancement in this field has come from being able to put humans into a fMRI machine and watch, in real-time, what areas of the brain are being stimulated.

The fMRI machine was invented in 1990 by Bell Laboratories and was a giant leap forward in helping us to understand how the brain processes information. fMRI stands for 'functional magnetic resonance imaging' and can measure brain activity in real time. This can provide a visual representation of which parts of the brain are being triggered as people undergo tasks, listen, and view information.

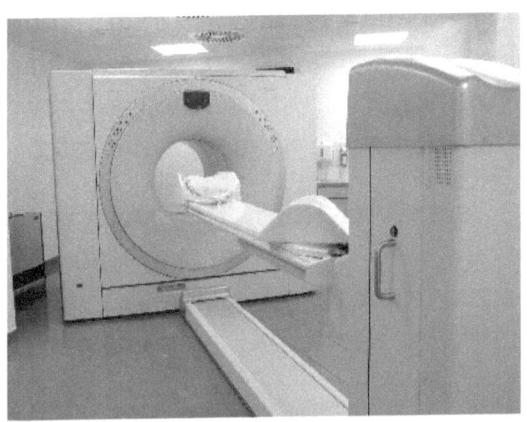

Neuroscience is the science that has come out of the study of the nervous system and seeks to understand the biological basis of behavior.

My first encounter with the power of the fMRI machine came in 2012 when I by chance came across a researcher from Israel, Eric Feingold of Feingold Technologies. Feingold had developed an algorithm that could predict the effectiveness of a sales message by examining only the tone of voice of a person presenting.

The way the algorithm was developed was by putting subjects into fMRI machines and then testing different messages and recording which parts of the brain lit up.

They sampled a million messages and found that the resulting algorithm was an accurate predictor of successful sales communication. It was a fascinating example of the power of neuroscience and how it could be applied to help people be more successful.

Influential Israeli-American psychologist Daniel Kahneman (THINKING FAST AND SLOW, 2011) showed how marketers could use brain research to speak directly to the subconscious and influence buying decisions.

Understanding how the brain works and how it has evolved is essential to understanding how to influence and connect better with people. The goal of your brand statement should be to trigger the right areas of the subconscious to influence positively the perception people have of you.

THE PARTS OF THE BRAIN

We can divide the brain into roughly two systems, which Kahneman termed simply as system 1 and system 2.

THE SYSTEM 1 BRAIN

System 1 is our automatic and nonconscious brain and is always on to protect us from perceived threats. It is often referred to as the "lizard brain" or "old brain" because it is that brain that has evolved from our most primitive ancestors. It is the *fast decision maker*.

System 1 is responsible for basic functions such as our heartbeat, breathing, and walking. Even talking and language are part of our system 1 lizard brains. Just imagine if you had to spend the time to process the act of taking a single step or saying a single word and you understand that these automatic brain functions are necessary.

The place where we get in trouble with our system 1 brains is in making near instantaneous assessments of people and situations based on incomplete information. In less than .07 of a second the system 1 brain determines threat or no threat.

Many of us refer to this feeling as our "gut feeling" and neuroscience has shown that this is something that is real. We have a strong neural connection between our guts and our brain, and this connection influences our emotions.

We relied on our gut feelings in the past to help protect us from predators and those that would seek to do us harm. Imagine being on the savannah of Africa and a person or wild animal running full speed towards you. You didn't have time to use your system 2 logical brain to evaluate the danger this situation presented to you. Your S1 brain made it for you and tended to always error on the side of caution.

The implications of this near-instantaneous gut feeling decisions in the modern world is profound. It is impossible to get all the relevant information about a person in the modern-day world in .07 seconds. We inevitably get it wrong and end up judging a person as a threat when in fact we have just misread the signals.

As an example, think of how to use your body language to signal to your neighbors you are not a threat. When you see them from afar, you nod your head and raise your eyebrows, which is a universal signal you will not harm them. Even the common handshake is a gesture for showing you are not carrying a weapon, and the drink toast (you splash your wine and mix them), showing that the wine has not been poisoned.

When you are writing your brand statement, you want to be sure you do the literary equivalent of these "I'm not a threat" signals. You want to be sure you are not saying something that can be interpreted as dangerous. It may sound obvious, but it is harder than you think.

Try this exercise. Read the following sentences aloud with different tones. Grab a partner and try it with them for the full effect.

I didn't say she loved me.
I **DIDN'T** say she loved me.
I didn't **SAY** she loved me.
I didn't say **SHE** loved me.
I didn't say she **LOVED** me.
I didn't say she loved **ME**.

You can take anything that people write and turn it around to something negative just by adding tone. Tone is why we get in so much trouble with our written digital communications. We look at emojis as just a way of adding fun to a message, but their purpose is much more. Emojis can help us communicate tone to people rather than leaving it to the reader to blindly determine our tone and intent.

In a groundbreaking 2013 STUDY BY HANNAH GACEY AND JIM GALLO, they asked 152 business professionals to read an email message with and without smiley emoticons. Here are examples:

I can't make the meeting you scheduled because it conflicts with my staff meeting. Email me and let me know what I missed.

vs.

I can't make the meeting you scheduled because it conflicts with my staff meeting. Email me and let me know what I missed. :-)

When questioned about what they read, the results showed that the message with the emoticon reduced significantly the negative tone of the message.

I am not suggesting that you fill your brand statement with emoticons, but you should think carefully about the tone you are projecting. Try reading it with different tones and see how it sounds. Remember that if you are unfortunate and end up having your statement read by a person having a bad day, they are likely to read negative tone into it. What you want is a statement that is impossible to be interpreted as negative. Ideally, you would like your statement to change their mood and put that smiley face on their face.

Another study – this one by neuroscientist DR. PAUL ZAK and digital and engagement strategy director Uwe Gurshow of Innocean – looked at people's emotional connections to brands to see if they could rival the emotional connection we have to people. Surprisingly they found that it was possible for a person to have a higher emotional response to a brand than to a loved one in their lives. Importantly, they found that the connection was only stronger when tied to a story. For example, one subject had a higher emotional response to a watch brand he loved than to his girlfriend. When investigating deeper why this was the case it was revealed that the watch was given to him by a beloved grandfather.

When considering how to present yourself, always keep the power of the story in mind. Stories resonate with our evolved brains and make social interactions rewarding. Your goal should be to develop an engaging story of who you are and what you can do.

THE SYSTEM 2 BRAIN

The System 2 brain is our slow-thinking brain. It is responsible for our cognitive functions, solving equations and thinking logically about things. It takes time to evaluate information and makes decisions based on the information provided. But it is painful work for us humans.

One significant truth about human beings is that our brains constantly look for shortcuts. We don't like to think long and hard about things and are more comfortable relying on our system 1 lizard brains to do the work for us.

Let me demonstrate how your brain works. Take this math problem:

$$2\left[3(4+7)-2(6-3)\right]$$

Most of us can solve this equation without too much difficulty which means our brains did not have to work too hard or use too much energy.

But if we take a more involved thought problem, you start to see how lazy our brains are.

Question: You are running a race with 3 people. If you pass the second to the last person, what place are you in? First? Second? Or third?

Many of us find this word problem frustrating. Our bodies will even react by our heart rate going up and our muscles tensing. Why? Because our brains are wired to look for shortcuts. In pre-historic times, we spent most of our days desperately trying to find enough calories to survive. When our bodies are starved of energy, we look for ways to conserve by limiting functions that are unnecessary. Our brains have evolved to be "lazy" and look for the shortest possible routes. Therefore, we prefer to just take the snap judgment of our system 1 lizard brain, our "gut feeling", and go with that.

When writing your brand statement, it is wise to remember the brains preference for the easy solution. Don't make people work too hard to understand who you are, make it simple for them to see you as a competent and kind person.

What is even more surprising from the research is even when we get our system 2 brain involved in thinking logically, it prefers to rely on the information it received from the system 1 lizard brain. What happens is the lizard brain makes a quick decision, and then the logical brain tries to connect facts to the "feeling" it gets to justify it was right.

I know some of you are getting stressed about the answer to the previous word problem. Your "lazy" brain is making you feel bad not having the answer, so I will give you the answer – you are in second place. Can you feel first the stress and annoyance, and then the relief when you get the easy answer? This is how your brain shows you it dislikes expending energy on things it deems unnecessary.

I have coached many salespeople over the years, and this is one of the key points I try to get them to understand. It is not about telling all the logical reasons about why someone should buy your product or service. It is about first getting the system 1 lizard brain to see you as someone that will help and not hurt them. That is how the buying decision is made; it is only after they have system 1 lizard brain approval that they move to the logical brain to justify why they want to buy from you.

If we think of the impact you want to make with your brand statement, the most essential element is to appease the system 1 lizard brain. The mistake people make in their statements on LinkedIn and on their resumes and CVs is listing just facts about what they have accomplished. They think people are logical and that they want to hear what they can do. But it is very important to always remember this quote from USC PROFESSOR OF NEUROSCIENCE ANTONIO DAMASIO:

"We are not thinking machines. We are feeling machines that think."

Focus your brand on the feeling part first and then add the logical to support the feeling you created.

North Carolina State University researcher Roger Myer and Purdue University researcher DAVID SHOORMAN found that you need to score well on integrity and honesty in order to positively connect with people. The four qualities necessary to score high are the 4Cs:

Capability: I believe you have the appropriate knowledge and skills (i.e. you possess competence, knowledge and ability that make me trust you).

Caring: I believe you are on my side (i.e. you display empathy, warmth and caring about my wants and needs).

Candor: I believe you will act with honesty and integrity (i.e. you will follow through on your promises and not deceive me).

Consistency: I believe you will act in a predictable and reliable manner (i.e. you behave in a dependable manner that minimizes surprises).

When creating your brand statement, keep in mind these 4Cs and be sure you are hitting on as many of them as you can.

People when reading your statement should be able to answer these two simple questions:

Why would anyone want to spend every day working with you?

How are you going to help the company – and more importantly me – to be more successful?

Friendliness and competence in balance – this is the key. Accomplish that in your statement and you will build higher levels of trust and more faith in your abilities.

WHAT IS TRUST?

Trust is simply a chemical that is released in our brain giving us a feeling of connection with others. Dr. Paul J. Zak is the neuroscientist responsible for showing that the hormone and neurotransmitter oxytocin is present also in close, trusting, working relationships.

Before Zak's work, oxytocin was thought to be only present in the bonding between mother and child. But Zak found oxytocin was also produced and exchanged between persons in close working relationships where high levels of trust existed. Oxytocin not only was exchanged but was responsible for making trust more difficult to break in those groups.

From an evolutionary perspective it makes sense for the human body to produce chemicals that support closer relationships. The reason humans were able to survive was because we were a species that was able to cooperate and help one another. Without trust it is impossible to collaborate and engage in activities that benefit the group, promote safety and lead to a higher probability of survival.

The definition of trust can be stated simply as:

The cumulative time that people do not spend in verifying others' actions and intentions.

WHAT DOES TRUST FEEL LIKE?

In Paul Thagard's book, _Mind-Society_, he proposes that trust is a brain process that binds representations of self, other, situation, and emotion into a special pattern of neural firing called a semantic pointer. This semantic pointer is created for each individual and is a result of the individual neural patterns that are created based on experience and stored memories. We form a cognitive appraisal and decide if trust is warranted and for what situations.

For leaders, it is important to remember that each person generates their own unique representation of situations and emotions and combine them to form the feeling of trust, or not.

Trust can be purely emotional, but most of the time trust involves both the emotion (S1) and logic (S2) parts of your brain. When people say they trust you, it is based on how they feel about you as well as their perceived prediction of how you will behave in the future.

Trust is also situational. For example, you might trust Bob to drive you to work, but you wouldn't trust Bob to perform heart surgery.

Trust provides a sense of confidence and security in others. When you feel it, you believe others will support and protect you. You believe people will do what they say and treat you fairly and with respect.

THE BUSINESS CASE FOR TRUST

Trust is the most important element of any working relationship and has been shown to have a direct impact on the success of the organization.

In an independent study of Fortune 100 Best Companies to Work For, found organizations with engaged and involved employees are significantly more likely to retain key talent than organizations with less employee trust. High-trust organizations experience up to 50% less turnover in staff than their competitors.

Looking at the results over the past 10 years, Trust Index scores and profits are also highly correlated. Where the Trust Index survey rises by more than half, profits increase twelvefold.

This not just a Western phenomenon. In a study, by Great Place to Work, in India found that a portfolio of India's Best Workplaces outperformed the Indian stock market indices by a factor of nearly four during a five-year period (2009-2013).

A four year-research project by Alex Edmans of the London Business School found employee well-being preceded positive financial performance, rather than the other way around.

Neuroscience researcher Paul J. Zak found that companies in the highest quartile of trust earned $6,450 (or 17%) more each year than employees at companies in the lowest quartile. According to Zak, "The only way this can occur in a competitive labor market is if employees in high-trust companies are more productive and innovative."

WHAT BUILDS TRUSTFUL RELATIONSHIPS

Building trust is a process and it takes time and relentless effort. I want to stress the word relentless here because it is important to remember it takes much time and effort to establish trust and only a moment to destroy it.

Exceptional leaders understand that every interaction with others is an opportunity to reaffirm the trust that has been established and move it to a higher level. Being *relentless* about trust building and nurturing should be the primary mission of every leader.

It can be argued that the key to building trustful relationships lies in the ability to predict others' behavior. The elimination of uncertainty in knowing how another person will behave is one of the cornerstones of high-trust relationships.

Remember our definition of trust: "The cumulative time that people do not spend in verifying others' actions and intentions." When you fully trust a person, you can with confidence predict how they will act. Leaders who are consistent in their actions and how they treat others score higher on the trust scale simply because those they lead can predict their behaviour more easily.

One of the leading causes of stress at work is uncertainty. When we are unsure and lack confidence in those we work with and for, it raises stress levels. Stress is not only bad for our health, but it also prevents us from collaborative and productive work.

By opening yourself up to how you like to work and what is important to you, you help others to better predict how you will behave, lowering their stress levels and creating an atmosphere of safety.

THE RESEARCH ON WHAT CONNECTS

According to Harvard Professors Amy Cuddy and Princeton Psychologist Susan Riske worldwide there are two factors that people judge you on: if you are friendly and well-intentioned, and competence or can you deliver what you promise.

People that are both friendly and competent are perceived by the brain to not be a threat and we are inclined to help them. People who demonstrate the opposite are people we respond contemptuously towards. Surprisingly those who are a mix, warm but not competent, elicit feelings of pity, while those who are perceived as competent but not warm provoke envy.

Psychologist Nicolas Kervyn, found that when people were presented with facts about two groups of people, one warm and one cold, the participants tended to assume that the warm group was less competent than the cold group. Likewise, if participants knew one group to be competent and the other not, they asked questions whose answers confirmed their hunch that the first group was cold and the second warm. The consequence: "Your gain on one [trait] can be your loss on the other," says Kervyn.

Balancing competence and warmth are vital to projecting the right perception. A long list of accomplishments in past jobs, or in school, may heighten your perception as being competent, but it will not support the idea you are friendly. The opposite is also true. If you only talk about how you want to save the planet, work selflessly for the betterment of humankind, or the only thing that matters is your family, you may score high on the warm and friendly scale, but people will question your abilities.

THE CONNECTION BETWEEN TRUST AND PSYCHOLOGICAL SAFETY

The term psychological safety goes back to 1965 and the book "Personal and Organizational Change Through Group Methods: The Laboratory Approach." Authors Schein and Bennis define it as a climate "which encourages provisional tries and which tolerates failure without retaliation, renunciation, or guilt."

In 1990, researcher Willian Kahn rejuvenated psychological safety and published an influential paper where he proposed psychological safety affects individuals' willingness to "employ or express themselves physically, cognitively, and emotionally during role performances," rather than disengage or "withdraw and defend their personal selves." Kahn argued that people are more likely to believe they will be given the benefit of the doubt—a defining characteristic of psychological safety—when relationships within a given group are characterized by trust and respect.

Harvard researcher Amy Edmondson in the late 90s defined it as the belief that the workplace is safe for interpersonal risk taking. Edmondson explained that it

31

is not about being nice, but about giving candid feedback, openly admitting mistakes, and learning from each other. It is only when this exists in a team can organizations perform better.

Edmondson's research was done with medical surgical teams involved in life and death situations daily. What she found was those teams that had a high degree of psychological safety had higher rates of patient survival. A shocking and telling fact.

But the story of the rise of psychological safety does not end here. It was Google, the giant US Internet search company, that is mostly responsible for the growth in the interest of psychological safety.

In 2011 Google undertook a study to try to understand what factors were responsible for high performance in its teams. It was well known in the 90s that Google only hired the best of the best people and the belief was that the more smart people you stick together, the higher performing the team will be. However, as researchers in Google observed how their teams worked together and the results they produced, they were not able to draw any statistical significance matching intelligence with team performance.

They went on to test a few more hypotheses. Was it diversity? Did those teams with more diversity (age, sex, ethnicity), perform better? No. What about social interaction? Did those teams who socialized outside of work achieve more results? But that also proved to be statistically insignificant. Researchers were at a loss to explain what made the difference until they stumbled on psychological safety.

Team observers noticed higher performing teams had a higher degree of trust and they supported one another actively in meetings. Higher performing teams made sure everyone contributed to the conversations they had.   They made an extra effort to include everyone.   They had a higher degree of emotional intelligence. At the same time the speaking between team members (measured in minutes of contribution) was, astonishingly, almost exactly evenly split between all the members.

At the same time, higher performing teams had a high degree of dependability ensuring that the work they did was done to a high level and on time. Team members could trust one another and didn't have to spend their time in verifying the actions and intentions of their fellow team members.

The differences between teams in performance was an incredibly significant 19%. Those teams that had a high degree of psychological safety outperformed their

KPIs (key performance indicators) by 19% while those teams who had a low level of psychological safety underperformed by 19%.

Google had their answer to what made a high performing team and proceeded to work to build psychological safety into all their teams.

Luckily for the world, Google shared their findings and made some of their research available to everyone interested in developing high performing teams. For the research and more background, you can visit Google's dedicated website re:Work at https://rework.withgoogle.com/

Google awoke the world to the idea of psychological safety as a corner stone of organizational performance and threw Amy Edmonson into the spotlight – even she had nothing to do with Google's research.

HOW DO YOU CREATE PSYCHOLOGICAL SAFETY?

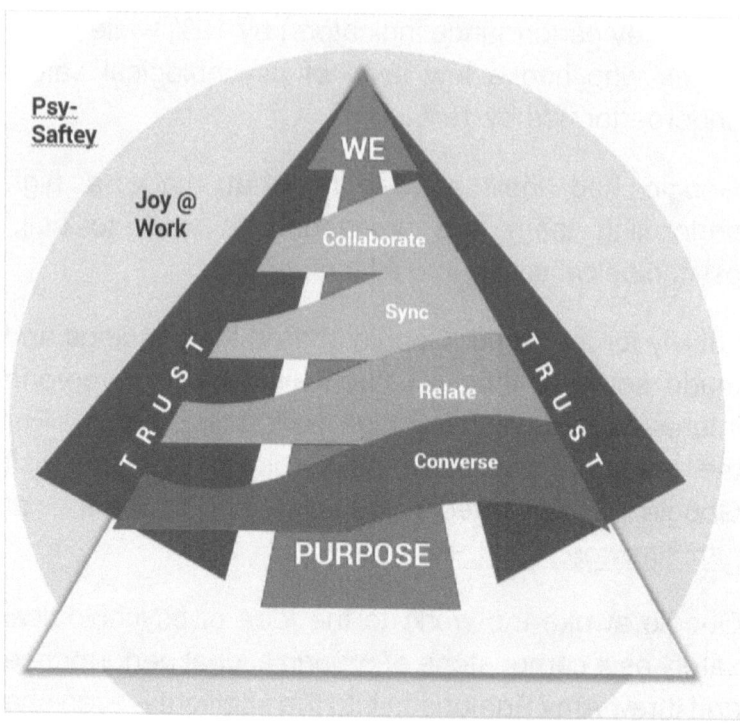

These are the steps in creating a psychologically safe team. It all starts with conversations.

CONVERSATIONS are fundamental to all human interactions. Developing Conversational Intelligence (C-IQ) helps you to up-regulate the positive and down-regulate the negative to drive higher levels of trust with those you work with.

Humans are hard-wired for **RELATIONSHIPS.** The brain is wired to look for signals that others appreciate us and our efforts. By building relationships and being social with others you foster meaningful connections and build a culture of mutual respect and dependence.

When humans agree their brains are in physical **SYNCHRONIZATION.** Neurons in our brains fire together when we agree with others. The better we paint the vision of a future together, the more the possibility exists for our brains to physically sync.

COLLABORATION happens only when we feel safe. People bring the best version of themselves to work and are fully engaged with what they are doing only when they feel safe. It is only through safety we can fully take advantage of collaboration.

WE-Centric thinking unleashes our potential to achieve more. When we embrace the view that every party brings value to an exchange, we shift from being adversaries to being co-creationist unleashing the power of the collective mind and moving from "my success" to "our success."

When we have all 5 conditions for psychological safety, the results are trust. Through high levels of trust, we are able with our teams to create greater purpose and understand how our work together creates value.

When we have purpose and trust we experience joy at work. We look at each day as an opportunity to learn from one another and open the possibility to achieving more and find ourselves in an environment of psychological safety. Free to bring our best self to work each day, support our colleagues, and harness the full power of out mental and physical self to the work at hand.

BUILDING A LEADERSHIP BRAND STATEMENT

INSPIRATIONAL BRAND STATEMENTS

I want to start by showing you a few brand statements from individuals who have made a name for themselves. The idea is to provide you with some inspiration and show you how a mix of warmth and competency can be effective in the real world.

The first example I want to show you is from Madeleine Albright. Former US Secretary of State and US Ambassador to the United Nations, she could speak only of her impressive political achievements and most would be satisfied. But Mrs. Albright has a great sense of what warmth means and its importance to connecting with people. Let's look at her Twitter profile.

Twitter is a tough place to get your branding just right due to the limited space you have. But her profile is a shining example of what can be accomplished.

She Writes:

> "Grateful American, Czech immigrant, mother & grandmother, fmr SecState, passionate democrat, author, prof, bizwoman, pin collector & occasional drummer."

Let's break down her statement so you can see the elements of warmth and competence in it.

First, the warmth elements. Being grateful to be an American is a statement meant to open our eyes to her views on what it means to be an American. As an immigrant, she found all the opportunities to reach the highest level of success in the United States, something that would have been impossible in the communist controlled Czechoslovakia of the post WWII era.

Next, she focuses us on the fact she is a mother and grandmother. Again, she is humanizing herself. We all have mothers and grandmothers and can relate to her in this personal way.

Now it is time for her to tell us about her competencies. Former US Secretary of State, author, professor, and business woman. These all tell us a lot about who she is and her abilities. Not to mention it makes us want to learn more about her and what she has done, something we all would like to motivate people to do with our own statements.

She throws in a quirky little side note within those accomplishments, "passionate democrat," meant to humanize herself. Political affiliations are risky for you to include in your statement, unless you work in an organization that is strongly politically affiliated. For Madeleine, is a part of who she is and her political life so not a problem.

Finally, she focuses us back on her warmth in a clever way. She mentions she is a pin collector and an occasional drummer. Wow – sorry but this just blows me away. Here is one of the most accomplished women in modern politics and she is using the limited character space on her Twitter profile to tell us these two ostensibly innocent facts. But think about it... Doesn't it make her so much more approachable? Can you picture her with a hat full of pins at some pin collector event? Or behind the kit knocking out a killer backbeat? I must admit that I struggled with that image, but it is something that intrigued me. Being a drummer myself it was something that hit me close to the heart.

It is an amazing example of the power of warmth and competency in balance.

Next is author and Ted Talk phenomenon Simon Sinek. Simon is a bestselling author and key note speaker. He talks common sense leadership and ideas that motivate and inspire people to work better together.

In his LinkedIn he describes himself as...

> "I imagine a world where almost everyone wakes up inspired to go to work, feels trusted and valued during the day, then returns home feeling fulfilled, like they have contributed to something greater than themselves. My team

> and I believe in this bright future and our ability
> to build it together."

Let's break down his statement and see why it is a good example of a brand statement.

First Simon, uses one of the most powerful words in sales, "imagine." When you ask people to imagine something you are not asking them to commit to buy or to give anything, you are only asking them to think about what it is you are saying. Here he is asking us to think about a world where we are inspired to go to work, where we feel trusted and valued. Powerful stuff.

He goes on to speak about returning home feeling fulfilled in having accomplished something greater. Again, isn't this what we all would like of our jobs? Simon is setting himself up as the one that can help us all to understand how to accomplish this.

Lastly, he connects us to his team. He is not in this alone, right? It takes others to execute on such a grand vision and he remembers to include them.

Another good example of a compelling brand statement comes from Jenny Blake. Jenny is an intriguing woman from New York who has built a successful blog, and is an author, speaker and coach. She is known for helping others "Wake up, live big, and love the Journey."

Let's look at her branding statement from the first page of her website at pivotmethod.com

> "I'm an author, speaker, career coach and business strategist living in New York City. I love helping awesome people like you organize your brain, move beyond burnout and build a sustainable career you love.

I'm fascinated by strategies for navigating change in our rapidly-evolving economy, and I geek out exploring and creating systems at the intersection of mind, body and business. I live for helping smart, talented, optimistic people like you embrace chaos, fear, insecurity and uncertainty as doorways of opportunity."

After a quick overview of what she does, Jenny moves on to what drives her and why it should matter to us. She loves helping "awesome" people like us to organize our brains and move ourselves and careers to the next level. Jenny addresses us as "smart, talented, and optimistic." Whether we are or not, does not matter. Don't we all like to think we aspire to be these things?

This is a great example of a brain-friendly statement that connects on a personal level and even succeeds in complimenting the reader. Jenny has already demonstrated her coaching abilities in her statement by making us come away feeling better even before we have met her.

A final example comes from Ivar Kroghrud, lead strategist at QuestBack.

"I am patient, even-tempered and easygoing. I appreciate straight, direct communication. Say

The User Manual of Me

what you are thinking and say it without wrapping your message.

I am goal-oriented but have a high tolerance for diversity and openness to different viewpoints. So, again, say what you are thinking and don't be afraid to challenge the status quo.

I welcome ideas at any time, but I appreciate that you have real ownership of your idea and that you have thought it through in terms of total business impact."

In the first sentence Ivar uses three words to describe how he controls his emotions – patient, even-tempered, and easygoing. He wants to control our perception of him as a person that has time for us and the patience to deal with difficult situations.

He then goes on to say that he values straight talk – say what you are thinking and don't "wrap" your message. This is extremely insightful for those working with Ivar. Like many Scandinavians (he is from Norway) he values direct conversations that do not talk around the issue. When working with him, it would be important to think how to be efficient in your communications.

The next paragraph he again stresses his respect for straight talk also adding that he welcomes people who challenge the status quo. He goes on to tell his appreciation for new ideas, but he wants you to show you have ownership of them and have considered closely the impact to the business.

From these few sentences you can see the great insight you now have into working with Ivan. You can see what is important to him and what he values. By Ivan sharing this with people he works with he manages to shorten the learning curve to successfully working with him. Effectively, he provides us with a short-cut to working better with him. Without this, we would jump into a team together and then spend a lot of time trying to guess what is important to him and how to best communicate.

By being honest with yourself in what you value, and communicating that simply to others, you provide insight and inspiration to others to work better with you.

Example Brand Statements

The brand statement is important for those that are in positions of leadership within organizations. In my 20+ years of developing leaders in multinational companies, it has become clear that having a leadership brand statement can go a long way towards building trustful relationships and breaking down barriers to working better together.

Zenger and Folkman researched 51,836 leaders around the world and found two factors that determine if a person is perceived as being a good leader; warmth and competence. That's right, it is the same two that the Harvard researchers found that people judge one another on. The title "boss" it does not bring with it respect, trust or belief in abilities. Those are things that must be cultivated and nurtured with people.

Just as it is essential to show your ability to do the job by taking on challenging projects, or solving business problems, it is as necessary to be proactive, even strategic, in expressing warmth. Empathy towards those you work with and those you lead is essential to creating your perception as a competent leader who can be trusted.

A well written personal brand statement gives you the possibility to define how you view others and how you want to work and lead them. It is the opportunity to open the doors to a better conversation with others, and it is through better conversations that we reveal our warmth and reinforce trust.

Let's look at some examples of brand statements to see in practice how to execute.

LEADERSHIP BRAND STATEMENTS

Example statements are from actual people who have used the brand tool. To protect their privacy, we do not disclose names or companies.

1. I'm an open, creative and organized leader. I trust in the power of a good group spirit and look for consensus in decision making. I drive things forward.
2. I am a thoughtful and energetic leader who promotes learning, creativity, and practical teamwork to efficiently achieve goals. I am known for being steady, level-headed, and kind in my decision making. I value close relationships and collaboration along with using knowledge and creativity to lead and motivate a team.
3. I am a leader who is always looking for new ways to improve our working methods and

processes to help improve the everyday life of others. I have experience from many parts of the company which provides me with an excellent picture of how things are done and insight into what could be improved. I treat people equally and I am always open to new ideas. I value learning through challenges. Challenges are opportunities to re-evaluate our current state and see if there is room for improvements.

4. I am a reliable, committed and a thoughtful leader who believes in helping our customers find solutions to improve their operations. I am known for following tasks through to completion and developing excellent customer relationships. I am open-minded, hardworking, and flexible in my work relations with others. I believe providing high-quality products sets us apart from our competitors. A good team spirit is vital to our success.

5. I am a logical, analytic, and team-oriented person who values independence and creative thinking. I am flexible in my approach to how the team meets its goals and considerate of new ideas and ways of working. I value accountability and believe setting measurable baselines and targets before work has begun will lead to the most significant success.

6. Experienced program manager with proven success in deploying IT solutions to enable transformations at leading global companies in challenging environments. Proficient at collaborating across boundaries in a distributed matrix organization to secure end-to-end execution. Known for having a highly structured approach and perseverance in delivering solutions to clients.

What do these statements have in common? They all express with authenticity what the author values and how they like to work. However, each is unique in what they reveal about the person.

Each statement opens the conversation on how to work better with that individual. Take for example the first brand, the individual values creativity but only when organized. There is a subtle but important difference between saying "I value creativity" and "I value creativity and organization." Can you spot the difference?

For this person, creativity needs to be controlled. Some might argue that this is not pure creativity but knowing this about the person helps to understand better how to work with them. They are open to new ideas, but you must present them in a way that is well thought out.

Let's look at another example. The person in statement 4 is customer focused and looks for solutions that best support the customer. Every statement in this brand is about the customer and how the work they do helps them. When working with this individual, it would be important to take this high level of customer focus into consideration. What could you do to support better customer service and fulfillment of customer needs?

Can you see how valuable your statement can be in a leadership situation? Going back to warmth as a leadership quality, when you take the time to express what is important to you in working with others, you demonstrate you care about them and succeeding together. How many times have we worked with people and just found it very difficult to understand what they want and what is driving them? Help others get that understanding of you, and you will forever change how they look and interact with you.

EXPERT/TEAM LEADERSHIP BRAND STATEMENTS

Example statements are from actual people who have used the brand tool. To protect their privacy, we do not disclose names or companies.

When writing a brand statement for working with others your brand works better if you take into consideration the different dynamic of leading but not supervising.

Let's look at some examples of these types of brands.

1. I am a resourceful expert in my field who believes in helping my co-workers and clients achieve their goals. I am known for my humor and compassion which provides comfort and promotes trust. I own my challenges and failures and will take accountability for my work, my product and my team. I value imagination, resourcefulness, and trust and I believe these are the values of successful leaders. I revel in being a dependable problem solver for my group and my clients.

2. I am an experienced technical thinker who can work across multiple disciplines and can spot and promote synergy among my colleagues in and out of my immediate organization. I can communicate technical concepts to individuals outside the specialized domains in which I work. At the same time, I can translate the interests of such people into the technical terms often required for significant advances. This often leads to innovative solutions to the most troublesome problems. My goal is to recognize

the interests and abilities of my peers (internal and external) and to promote them. Inclusiveness is a priority for me, and I work to expose talent across the organization.

3. I am energetic, reliable, and focused on the team's goals and objectives. I am known for being honest and direct and try to lead by example. I enjoy collaboration and value other people's perspectives and knowledge. I deeply value communication, openness, and honesty and believe these are essential to a team's potential. I'm customer focused and always looking for ways to improve myself.

4. I am an experienced software engineer who loves solving challenging problems that require creativity and application of new skills and knowledge. I have a proven track record planning and leading the successful development of new products on tight timelines and budgets, often despite ambiguous requirements and unanswered technical questions. I take great pride in my work and am not satisfied until I have shipped robust code that will serve as a steady foundation for future development.

5. I'm interested in learning and development of new things. I want to find out new ways to work

and collaborate with others. I like challenges and problem-solving. I value accountability and collaboration. A positive mindset is important to me and change should be an opportunity for development.

Dissecting these brands, we can see the tone is less direct. There is a difference in the relationship dynamics when you are not supervising a person. In these situations, it is imperative to express your ability to work with others well and what you bring that will help others to be successful.

If we take the first statement, from George (not his real name) a young technical engineer, as an example, the author has highlighted several important aspects that demonstrates how he is valuable to the team. Let's break down his statement.

I am a resourceful expert in my field (2) who believes in helping my co-workers and clients achieve their goals. (3) I am known for my humor and compassion which provides comfort and promotes trust. (4) I own my challenges and failures and will take accountability for my work, my product and my team.

The first sentence (1) tells the reader he is a qualified expert in his field. This information is important for creating credibility and for showing the qualifications necessary to do the job. People must be able to trust in your ability to complete the job.

Next, is the statement that George believes it is important to help his co-workers and clients achieve their goals (2). He is committed to the success of others and works to assist his co-workers and clients in the achievement of their goals. We all want to believe our co-workers are devoted to mutual success. Being customer-focused is also extremely important to those you work with. Without customers none of us have a job. Affirming your focus on customers demonstrates to others you value customer success.

I always tell people I coach, those you work with want to know they are working with a human being and not a robot. In the third part (3), George is humanizing himself by describing a quality that people admire – his humor. We all like to work with people who are fun and have a good sense of humor. By stating that he has this quality and compassion, we get a strong sense he would be someone we would enjoy working with.

Lastly, George states his ability to own challenges and be accountable (4). A strong statement that hits at the heart of working well. Customers and companies want people who own up to their responsibilities and can be trusted not to shift blame to others.

George's statement is a brand that hits all the right areas for working with others. When you read it, you can feel your system 1 lizard brain telling you that this is a solid and competent person that would be enjoyable to work with.

USING THE BRANDING TOOL

PART ONE THE SURVEY

The branding tool is divided into 2 parts. The first part is a brief questionnaire that asks you to identify aspects of your personality, your strengths, challenges, and values. It is designed to help you think more deeply about yourself by asking questions to get to the core of who you are as a person.

Some of you may have taken personality or behavior assessments in the past, tools like the Myers-Briggs Type Indicator or the DISC behavior assessment. Our tool shares elements of those assessments, but its purpose is different. Its goal is not for clinical or psychological evaluation. The branding tool is for helping you to craft the ideal perception of you.

Perception is the key word to remember. The information you get from a psychological assessment, is of no importance when you are aiming to establish better relationships with those you work. It is within your power to create the perception you want others to have of you. Your darkest personality traits do not, and should not, be a part of this perception. We all have areas of ourselves we do not wish to share with others, and that is OK not to share them. What we want to share are the things about us that help others to understand the positive aspects of who we are.

THE JOHARI WINDOW – BLIND SPOTS

A useful way to look at the purpose of the branding tool is through the eyes of the Johari Window. The Johari window was developed by psychologist Joseph Luft and Harrington Ingham to help people understand the relationship with themselves and others. It divides the self into 4 quadrants. The first is the **Open** quadrant, the things everyone knows about you and you know about yourself. Things as simple as your sex, your age, your education, how tall you are, hair color, if you are married or single, etc.

The second quadrant comprises **Hidden** things, those things you know about yourself, but others do not see. We all have things we know about ourselves but do not feel comfortable sharing with others. It might be an insecurity or something we are embarrassed to admit. It is OK to have this **Hidden** area, everyone has one and it is normal and healthy.

The third quadrant is the **Blind Spot** and this comprises things others know about us, but we don't know about ourselves. We have all met people that have something about them that is holding them back, or not helping them to be successful and are just not aware of it. This is known as the **Blind Spot**.

 The last quadrant is the **Unconscious.** This is an area we don't know about ourselves and others also don't know. This area is only opened by professional counseling and is not part of our work here.

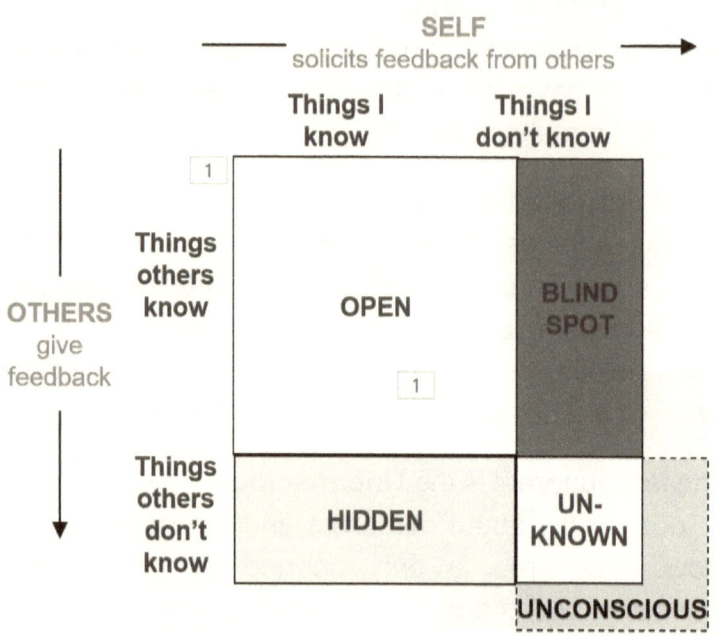

What is the goal here? The goal is to reduce the **Hidden** quadrant and the **Blind Spot**.

The brand tool can open the **Hidden** quadrant and possibly even the **Blind Spot** by helping you to take an honest look at yourself and what is important to you.

The questions in the first part of the tool, the survey part, are designed to help you explore the perception you have of yourself. It is not essential when you take the survey if the opinion you have of yourself is 100% accurate or if others share the same perception. It is best to answer the survey with complete honesty.

In part 2 I will take you step-by-step through the process of examining your results and determine if what you have chosen supports you in building a favorable perception, one other people find persuasive.

PART 2 OF THE BRAND TOOL – THE WORKSHEET

Get your own personalized worksheet by visiting https://createmybrand.us/ *and taking the survey. You will be emailed directly your results and the worksheet to complete.*

The second part of the brand tool is the brand worksheet. Its purpose is to take you step-by-step through your answers from part 1 and guide you through the process of analyzing your perceptions.

WHAT KIND OF PERSON ARE YOU?

Jeff Bezos, the founder of Amazon, is credited with saying "Your brand is what other people say about you when you're not in the room." What people say can be expressed by the formula:

Strengths + Talents +/- Behaviours = Value to those you serve

S + T + B = V

Behaviors can, and often are, a negative quantity that can inversely affect your perceived value.

The first part of the worksheet looks at how you think others perceive you. The survey asked you to pick one of four types as the one you believe have the characteristics that people would use to describe you.

This part of the survey is based on William Moulton Marston's DISC behavior assessment. DISC is a widely used assessment for helping determine your behavioral style. Some people like to refer to it as your personality, but technically your personality is a bit more complicated. But the types Marston developed are useful in describing your dominant personal behavior type.

The four types are (1) Dominance, (2) Influencer, (3) Steadiness and (4) Compliance (DISC). The numbers 1 to 4 represent the types in our survey and the worksheet results. You were asked to pick one as representing how you believe most people perceive you. Your choice is recorded in the "Your choice" area.

Your choice: TWO Enthusiastic, Persuasive, Animated, Energetic, Talkative, Spontaneous

Characteristics of the Four Types:

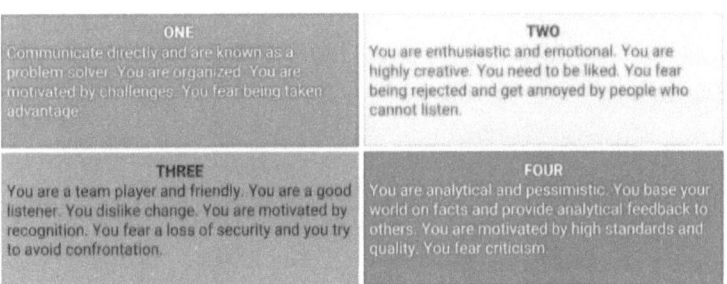

ONE	TWO
Communicate directly and are known as a problem solver. You are organized. You are motivated by challenges. You fear being taken advantage.	You are enthusiastic and emotional. You are highly creative. You need to be liked. You fear being rejected and get annoyed by people who cannot listen.
THREE	**FOUR**
You are a team player and friendly. You are a good listener. You dislike change. You are motivated by recognition. You fear a loss of security and you try to avoid confrontation.	You are analytical and pessimistic. You base your world on facts and provide analytical feedback to others. You are motivated by high standards and quality. You fear criticism.

The worksheet then provides an overview of all 4 and asks you to analyze if the one you chose is the one you think genuinely describes you and how you would like others to perceive you. How we are, and how we want people to view us are often two separate things.

Let's say you think people would describe you as a type one Dominant but you don't identify with that type. You see it as too hard and direct and you would prefer to be seen as softer and friendlier. Your brand statement could highlight your softer aspects to prime people's brains to look for your softer side and not your hard dominant side.

Priming the brain is a technique that is used by marketers to train your brain to look for specific information. Let me demonstrate how it works by recreating the famous priming experiment by Russian psychologist Alfred Lukyanovich Yarbus conducted in 1967.

Look at the following painting entitled 'The Unexpected Visitor'.

Now hide the image and answer the following question:

How many pictures are on the wall?

Now look back at the picture. Were you right? I am sure you got it very wrong. Why? Because your brain was not primed to look for that information. You were primed to look at the people in the painting. The title 'The Unexpected Visitor' primed your brain and focused your eye movements on the people in the room and what they are doing.

Applying this technique to your brand statement you can focus people on the things that you want them to "see" and avoid those that you do not want them to see.

It is important to remember that in many situations, such as in a job search, people have yet to meet you and have nothing to base their perception on. This means you have a blank page to help direct them towards the perception you want them to have of you.

Some might be concerned that we are being less than truthful with people if we are trying to sell ourselves as something we are not. Although this might be true, you need to remember the goal of your statement. Your brand is meant to express the ideal you, what you would like to be, how you would want to work, and what is important to you. It is up to you to live up to that ideal in how you conduct yourself.

You can look on it as an exercise in marketing and presenting yourself as a product in the best possible light. Think if product marketing only told the 100% truth, would we ever buy anything? Probably not. It is about how you present that product. Let's take for example a chocolate candy bar. It has lots of good and bad qualities and it is up to the marketer to highlight the good qualities and minimize the bad ones. To illustrate this point, look at the two examples here, which one would you buy?

Would you buy the one that is 90% fat-free or the one that has 10% fat? For most, the 90% fat free is more seductive, and this is how marketers frame their products. Does the candy bar have 10% fat? Yes, it does. But is that what the candy manufacturer wants you as the customer to focus on? No, it is not. Is the glass half full or half empty? A good marketer always wants the customer to see the glass as half-full.

Unfortunately, the brain has evolved to see the world as half-empty. It was being overly pessimistic that helped humans to survive. New situations, ways of doing things, people, were all risks to our survival and so the brain evolved to be overly pessimistic. For prehistoric man, taking risks got you killed.

It is your job to help people overcome this natural inclination to be pessimistic towards you by framing yourself in a way that focuses them on the positive, on your "90% fat-free."

YOUR IDENTIFIED CHARACTER STRENGTHS

The second part of the survey asks you to identify two signature strengths from a list of six. According to research carried out by former President of the American Psychological Association Martin Seligman and University of Michigan Professor Christopher Peterson, and published in the book Character Strengths and Virtues, we all have in us signature strengths which are broken down and defined as the following:

1. **Wisdom and Knowledge:** creativity, curiosity, open-mindedness, love of learning, perspective, and innovation.
2. **Courage:** bravery, persistence, integrity, vitality, and zest.

3. **Humanity:** love, kindness, social intelligence
4. **Justice:** citizenship, fairness, leadership.
5. **Temperance:** forgiveness and mercy, humility, prudence, and self-control.
6. **Transcendence:** appreciation of beauty and excellence, gratitude, hope, humor, and spirituality.

The worksheet provides your results with the two strengths you chose for yourself, in this format:

ONE - Creativity, Curiosity, Open-Mindedness, love of learning, providing wise learning to others

TWO - Bravery, persistence, integrity, approaching life with excitement and energy

The worksheet asks you to verbalize into a single statement how your strengths define you as a person.

POSSIBLE DERAILERS (BLIND-SPOTS) TO YOUR POSITIVE BRAND PERCEPTION

The third part of the worksheet looks at the things that could hold you back. I have included this for two reasons, one it is essential, to be honest with yourself about things that might stand in the way of your success. The second is for you to learn how to answer questions that inevitably come up about what you need

67

to improve in yourself or what you find challenging in interview situations. This section gives insight into those areas and offers an opportunity to reflect on what you can do to overcome them. I ask you to identify from a list 3 things. The results look like this:

You identified 3 things that you find challenging. Those three things are listed here:

let go and trust others with important tasks, keep my emotions in check when in stressful situations, listen to others when the way forward is so clear.

YOUR PERSONAL VALUES

Finally, I ask about your values. Values form the foundation of your personal truth. Knowing what we value helps us to make decisions and act to fulfill the life we want to live. If you know your values, it becomes easier to pick the correct direction. Helping others to understand your values provides insight to them in how and why they should work with you.

I provided in the survey a list of values to select from. I did not limit the number you could select but left it open to those that speak to you.

The results are presented like this on the worksheet:

You identified the following values as ones that you have a personal connection to:

Accomplishment, Creativity, Dependability, Diversity, Enthusiasm, Fairness, Growth, Impact, Optimism

The worksheet then asks you to prioritize those values and explain how they are important to you. I also ask you to think if those values would be known to those you work with, or would they come as a surprise, and why?

CRAFTING YOUR AUTHENTIC PERSONAL BRAND STATEMENT

The last part of the worksheet is to create, or craft, your personal brand statement. I hope at this point you have a clearer understanding of yourself and what is important to you.

The challenge now is to put everything together in a statement of around 75 words.

As a good starting point, I suggest that you divide your statement into 4 parts.

   (1) Statement of who you are.
   (2) What you offer.

(3) How your strengths help you achieve success.

(4) What you value and how that contributes to making you and those you work with more successful.

Let's examine the example from the worksheet to help you understand how to do this. The following is my personal brand statement and comes in at 75 words. The statement was built according to the survey results; my results are recorded above as the examples for each section.

My brand

(1) I am a creative, energetic, and persuasive person who believes in helping people and organizations to achieve more than they thought possible. (2) I am known for my innovative approaches which provide valuable insight and direction. (3) I am open-minded, fair, and flexible in my work relations. (4) I value diversity in all its forms and believe it is the path to greatness. Developing people is my passion. Coaching is a skill. Customers are my priority.

Go back and read my statement again in its entirety. Now try to imagine that you are thinking of hiring me for a job to help train and develop people.

Now do one quick exercise, turn over the paper and write three things you know about me. When you are done continue below.

What did you come up with? What words immediately came to mind about me? Did they match the core ideas in my brand statement? Was it easy to think of three things?

What feelings did you get when reading it? Did you feel I am a person you would like to work with? Did you get a warm and genuine sense I care for other people? Did I sound sincere in describing myself? Did your lizard brain relax and say, "maybe this guy could help me?" Did your system 2 brain think I have skills that would be useful in developing people?

I hope you got at least some of these feelings when reading this statement. I am not saying it is perfect and you would get these feelings, but I hope at least a few of them. I hope that my genuine desire to help people achieve came across strong and that you can identify a couple of my abilities.

Let's examine in depth my statement and see how I constructed it.

In the first sentence, I set out to accomplish 3 things:

1. Appease the system 1 lizard brain – show I am not a threat: "I help people"
2. Appease the system 2 brain by giving my key competencies: "I am creative, energetic, and persuasive"
3. Provide my competitive advantage: "I am a person who believes in helping people and organizations to achieve more than they thought possible"

In the second sentence, I work to reinforce my competencies and why they are useful to others: "I am known for my innovative approaches which provide valuable insight and direction."

The third and fourth sentences are again focused on the system 1 lizard brain, helping the reader to understand that I am a person that respects people: "I am open-minded, fair, and flexible in my work relations. I value diversity in all its forms and believe it is the path to greatness."

Finally, I connect my values and use it to summarize myself, and what I believe: "Developing people is my passion. Coaching is a skill. Customers are my priority."

I will admit that my statement took many revisions before I was happy with it. When you write your brand, it is good to do the first draft and then put it aside, even overnight is good. Then come back to it with fresh eyes and see does it have the message you want it to have.

Your statement also needs to evolve as you evolve as a person, it should be a living document. Revisit every six months and make adjustments.

CONCLUSIONS

To quote <u>William Bernbach</u>, one of the original Mad men:

> "Nothing is so powerful as an insight into human nature… what compulsions drive a man, what instincts dominate his action… if you know these things about a man you can touch him at the core of his being."

I hope that I have opened your mind and provided insight into the possibility of creating a unique brand statement that will touch people at the core of their being.

Answering the question of who I am is not an easy task, but one we need to answer if we are to create a work environment that builds trust and promotes psychological safety.

A well-formulated personal brand statement is the first step you can take to positively influence how others view you. Being able to then express that statement to those you work with will help to create the positive perceptions of you that will form a solid foundation for future success together.

ACTION VERBS

I have included here a list of action verbs that can be helpful to you when looking for words in building your brand statement. It can be a challenge to find the right words to describe your experience. I hope that this list provides a starting point to triggering your mind.

Leadership Skills	decided	hired
achieved	delegated	hosted
administered	developed	improved
analyzed	directed	incorporated
appointed	eliminated	increased
assigned	emphasized	initiated
attained	enforced	inspected
authorized	enhanced	instituted
chaired	established	led
considered	evaluated	managed
consolidated	executed	merged
contracted	expanded	motivated
controlled	generated	organized
converted	handled	originated
coordinated	headed	overhauled

oversaw

pioneered

planned

presided

prioritized

produced

recommended

reduced (losses)

reorganized

replaced

restored

scheduled

secured

selected

streamlined

strengthened

supervised

surpassed

terminated

**Communication/
People Skills**

addressed

advertised

arbitrated

arranged

articulated

authored

clarified

collaborated

communicated

composed

condensed

conferred

contacted

conveyed

convinced

corresponded

debated

defined

described

developed

directed

discussed

drafted

edited

elicited

enlisted

explained

expressed

formulated

furnished

influenced

interacted

interpreted

interviewed

involved

joined

judged

lectured

listened

marketed

mediated

moderated

negotiated

observed

outlined

participated

persuaded

presented

promoted

proposed

publicized

reconciled

recruited

referred

reinforced

reported

resolved

responded

solicited

specified

spoke

suggested

summarized

synthesized

translated

wrote

Problem-Solving

Skills

analyzed

clarified

collected

compared

conducted

critiqued

detected

determined

diagnosed

evaluated

examined

experimented

explored

extracted

formulated

gathered

identified

interpreted

invented

investigated

located

measured

organized

researched

reviewed

searched

solved

summarized

surveyed

tested

Technical Skills

adapted

applied

assembled

built

calculated

computed

conserved

constructed

converted

debugged

designed

determined

developed

engineered

fortified

installed

maintained

operated

overhauled

printed

programmed

rectified

regulated

remodeled

repaired

replaced

restored

solved

specialized

spearheaded

standardized

studied

upgraded

utilized

Teaching Skills

adapted

advised

clarified

coached

communicated

conducted

coordinated

critiqued

developed

enabled

encouraged

evaluated

explained

facilitated

focused

guided

informed

instilled

instructed

motivated

persuaded

set goals

simulated

stimulated

taught

tested

trained

transmitted

tutored

Financial/

Data Skills

administered

adjusted

allocated

analyzed

appraised	reduced	established
assessed	researched	fashioned
audited	retrieved	formulated
balanced	saved	founded
budgeted	**Creative Skills**	illustrated
calculated	acted	initiated
computed	adapted	instituted
conserved	began	integrated
corrected	combined	introduced
determined	composed	invented
developed	conceptualized	modeled
estimated	condensed	modified
forecasted	created	originated
managed	customized	performed
marketed	designed	photographed
measured	developed	planned
planned	directed	revised
prepared	displayed	revitalized
programmed	drew	shaped
projected	edited	solved
reconciled	entertained	wrote

Counseling Skills

adapted

advocated

assessed

assisted

cared for

clarified

coached

counseled

demonstrated

diagnosed

educated

encouraged

ensured

expedited

facilitated

familiarized

furthered

guided

intervened

mediated

mentored

motivated

prevented

provided

referred

rehabilitated

represented

resolved

simplified

supported

Organization/Detail Skills

approved

arranged

catalogued

categorized

charted

classified

coded

collected

compiled

corrected

corresponded

distributed

executed

filed

generated

implemented

incorporated

indexed

inspected

inventoried

logged

maintained

monitored

obtained

operated

ordered

organized

prepared

processed

provided

purchased

recorded	compiled	directed
registered	conceived	generated
reserved	created	improved
responded	designed	initiated
retrieved	developed	increased
reviewed	established	promoted
routed	formulated	reduced
scheduled	founded	Administrative
screened	influenced	Skills
set up	implemented	administered
submitted	initiated	approved
supplied	instituted	arranged
standardized	supported	coordinated
systematized	surveyed	designed
updated	tabulated	established
validated	updated	evaluated
verified	Time-	headed
Development Skills	Management	hired
analyzed	Skills	interpreted
applied	administered	interviewed
catalogued	developed	managed

mediated	completed	succeeded
negotiated	expanded	surpassed
organized	exceeded	transformed
prepared	improved	won
planned	pioneered	
supervised	reduced (losses)	
Additional Verbs for Accomplishments	resolved (issues)	
	restored	
achieved	spearheaded	

ADDITIONAL READING

Simone Kühn , Jürgen Gallinat, *Does Taste Matter? How Anticipation of Cola Brands Influences Gustatory Processing in the Brain*
http://journals.plos.org/plosone/article?id=10.1371/journal.pone.0061569

Read Montague, *Coke or Pepsi? It's all in the head*
https://www.theguardian.com/world/2004/jul/29/science.research

Thinking Fast and Slow by Daniel Kahneman: https://en.wikipedia.org/wiki/Thinking,_Fast_and_Slow

2013 study done by Hannah Gacey and Jim Gallo - *Some SCIENCE Behind the Smiley... Emoticons and Their Possible Impact on the Workplace:* http://www.hrfloridareview.org/item/266-some-science-behind-the-smiley-emoticons-and-their-possible-impact-on-the-workplace

Paul Zak, *How Stories Change the Brain:* https://greatergood.berkeley.edu/article/item/how_stories_change_brain

USC Professor of Neuroscience Antonio Damasio and his work with understanding emotion: https://en.wikipedia.org/wiki/Antonio_Damasio

David Shoorman, Interpersonal trust: http://www.krannert.purdue.edu/directory/bio.php?username=schoor

Amy Cuddy and Princeton Psychologist Susan Riske, *Mixed Impressions: How We Judge Others on Multiple Levels:* https://www.scientificamerican.com/article/mixed-impressions/

Nicolas Kervyn, *Competence and warmth in context: The compensatory nature of stereotypic views of*

national *groups.*
http://nicolaskervyn.blogspot.com/

Zenger and Folkman, *I'm the Boss! Why Should I Care If You Like Me?*
https://hbr.org/2013/05/im-the-boss-why-should-i-care

Joseph Luft and Harrington Ingham, The Johari Window
https://en.wikipedia.org/wiki/Johari_window

Christopher Pertersen and Martin Seligman, *Character Strengths and Virtues*
https://en.wikipedia.org/wiki/Character_Strengths_and_Virtues

William Bernbach, The original Mad Man of Advertising
https://en.wikipedia.org/wiki/William_Bernbach

Resources

All resources are freely available at the time of publication.

Take the accompanying survey to help you understand yourself better and get the personal workbook to assist in writing your brand statement: http://www.createmybrand.us

Check the readability of your statement – it is go to strike a balance between being easily understo (i.e. a lower-grade level) and intelligent (a higher-grac level). Depending on your audience adjust accordingly https://www.webpagefx.com/tools/read-able/

Check the tone of your statement using IBM's Watson supercomputer: https://tone-analyzer-demo.ng.bluemix.net/

Explore deeper your strengths and take the Via Institute on Character's free Strength Survey: https://www.viacharacter.org/

Understand your dominate personality type: Take the online DISC assessment: https://www.123test.com/disc-personality-test/

Me

od
od
e
.